YOU DON'T KNOW YOU NEED THIS BOOK
UNTIL YOU READ THIS BOOK

ATTRACTION & INTENTION

T.S. Olivares

Copyright © 2023 T.S. Olivares All rights reserved.

No part of this book may be reproduced, stored in a retrieval system, or transmitted in any form or by any means, electronic, mechanical, photocopying, recording, or otherwise, without express written permission of the publisher.

ISBN: 9798393432225
Imprint: Independently published

Cover designed by: Freelancer Rakib

Printed in the United States of America

First Edition

Dedication...

To all the like-minded and kindred spirits that have been doing everything within their power, to bring their best life to the table. I hope this information will help you see that all is possible and with the right guidance, the ability to create your future is truly within your grasp.

To my wife and partner who has inspired and sharpened me. She has been my rock and always provided me with the opportunity to grow and become the best version of myself.

TABLE OF CONTENTS

YOU DON'T KNOW i

    Dedication iii

    Preface 1

Introduction 11

PART I: Tools 15

    Chapter One: Intention 17

    Chapter Two: Attraction............................. 19

    Chapter Three: The Mind 22

    Chapter Four: Focus 26

PART II: APPLICATION 28

    Chapter Five: Laser Focus......................... 30

    Chapter Six: How to Begin 33

    Chapter Seven: The Inventory................... 37

    Chapter Eight: Gratefulness 38

    Chapter Nine: The Future.......................... 39

    Chapter Ten: Picking Your Goals 40

    Chapter Eleven: Cognitive Distortions...... 42

    Chapter Twelve: Life Script 44

    Chapter Thirteen: The Routine.................. 45

PART III: REFLECTIONS 48

    Surrender Early.. 50

    Unwavering Belief Required 53
    The Poison and the Antidote 55
    Big Goals – Little Goals 57
    Results 59
    Joy and the Ego 63
Epilogue 66
Bibliography 68
About The Author 69

Preface

"The Beginning is always today."
-Mary Wollstonecraft Shelley

Most of us spend the first half of our lives trying to figure out who we are, what we want, and why we are here. For many, happiness is elusive as we look outward to satisfy and feed an emptiness we feel inside.

As we peck through life like a chicken looking for seed, a few realize joy comes from inside, not the next cool gadget, iPhone, car, house, toy, or video game. Still, others take decades to figure it out. And yet some of us never find joy at all.

As we reach adulthood, still operating on the subconscious programs of a child, we see the world and ourselves with an inaccurate perception. We think, act, and react unconsciously and get in our own way. We see or think about what we want, but somehow, we never quite get there. The outward results in life are created by our thoughts and inherited beliefs. We operate like a computer with bad programming. The old computer saying, "garbage in - garbage out," is also relevant to our journey through life.

It is time to put away childish things and take control of our lives and our destinies. This book will get you on the right path and you will only know that you need this book once you read it.

Bad programming, phobias and fears cause physical reactions. Your body produces chemicals and hormones based on your feelings and emotions. Too much of anything is harmful, and the medical profession is connecting physical well-being with emotional well-being. All these things prevent us from finding true joy and a deeply satisfying life. This journey in 3-d consists of more than just getting a job, having a family, and playing follow the leader. Deep inside, everyone longs for joy and liberty. Many of us just settle.

Yet, no matter where you start, you can create an extraordinary life full of joy and accomplishment. We are limited by our self-image and our unconscious programming. Most of us are unaware of the things that drive our life and reality. Luckily, the programs are not fixed, and we can make changes. This book explains clearly how and where our programs came from and how we can alter them. In this book I introduce Laser Focus, a framework that can help to change things. If you are ready to move to the next level, then it is no coincidence you are reading this book.

I attempted to have a "normal" life and follow the program, but like Neo in the movie, "The Matrix," something was off. The single-minded quest for material things you can't take with you didn't make sense. It was tremendously unfulfilling. In my case, no matter what profession I got into, the satisfaction of the achievement left quickly. Before long, after mastering the job, I found myself needing to be more inspired. I wanted to be excited about my profession, continually challenged, and make a difference in the world. I rationalized that I just hadn't found my calling yet.

I still remember the words of my grandmother. God rest her soul. She accused me of having the "Peter Pan Syndrome." It was a label applied to someone who changes professions frequently. It compared job restlessness with the idea of a fictional character who never wanted to grow up, so he never got a job. This comes from when you spent your first 18-22 years in school, got married, had kids, and settled for a job working 40 hours a week for 40 years with the same company and then retired. That time is dead. Today people are looking for happiness and to take control of their destinies. Happiness does not come from lots of money. It comes from connecting with the ones we love, having enough to pay the bills and see this fantastic planet, reconnecting with nature, and creating liberty.

Even at a young age, I was looking for happiness and joy. In my teens, I remember brainstorming about the future. I wanted to start my own business, travel, save the whales, and figure out the meaning of life. I wanted to make a difference. I didn't even know where to start.

So, while being responsible and working a regular job, I would spend my downtime searching for the perfect life. I spent years getting more knowledge and information. I became convinced that we all can create the life we want. I dove into anything I could find on personal growth and development. I read over 100 different books by different authors and new-age thinkers. Many are still writing and teaching today. I wanted more than the status quo. I even went as far as to read about every religion looking for clues. I found no real answers in the faith I was baptized under, so why not look around. We have all had those moments when we ask, "Why do we get up every day and do the same things we did yesterday? What is the end game? Is there a bigger purpose for me?

I did make some headway. There was a common theme in all the literature. It became clear that everything in nature either decays and dies from inaction or expands and evolves to become part of something bigger. I did not like the sound of decay. I wanted to be part of something bigger. I wanted to evolve. Not like growing gills or another finger. We are talking about personal evolution. Personal evolution is a change of perspective, maturation, and shifting view of yourself in the world, your role in the world, and your life.

There are two ways to create a change or a personal evolution. One way to approach it is analytical. This involves focusing on our thinking, self-image, and subconscious programming. The other approach was emotional. It is believed that having an experience with a significant emotional impact gives birth to a new awareness that forces you to evolve.

My search led me to Dr. Maxwell Maltz's groundbreaking research first publish in 1960, in his book, "Psycho-Cybernetics." It went into great detail on the topic of subconscious reprogramming." Maltz was the first researcher and author to explain the power of the subconscious (mind) and how to reprogram it. He writes the process used to retrain the subconscious mind is called Auto-programming. It requires repetitive affirmations, goal setting, envisioning, and then allowing the "Subconscious Mind" to bring about changes. This reprogramming typically takes a minimum of 21 days of repetition, faith, and patience. So, to move forward, I would have to choose from the analytical approach, the emotional one or perhaps both. As the mysterious hand of fate would have it, the decision was made for me.

Shortly after moving to California, I was sponsored into an LGAT seminar offered by PSI seminars. PSI Seminars is a private company that offers large-group awareness training (LGAT) seminars for professional and personal development. Programs are held in the U.S., Canada, Japan, and worldwide. Many people leave the event supercharged, and the experience brings about positive change in their lives and businesses. Armed with a new view of creating our realities, many people take charge of a life they previously lived on automatic pilot. Jack Canfield, one of the co-authors of the Chicken Soup Books Series, refers to PSI in his book "The Success Principles." He credits them with having an impact on his life. I attended several workshops and spent a week at their Clear Lake Oaks, California ranch. This program had elements that addressed my analytical side while still providing me with an emotionally impactful experience. It would seem my evolution had begun. An important thing I learned is that we create our life through thinking. The most memorable catchphrase was "To think is to create." If you consider it carefully, you will agree that any item that humanity has produced started in the mind of its creator. You can only create something once you envision it. So, I started to envision or, more accurately, imagine the life I wanted to create.

The next pivotal moment in my growth was finding the book called "The Secret." It hit the bookshelves in 2006 and the movie came out later that year. It was an eye-opening story about creating your life using intention. The author Rhonda Byrne was heavily influenced by the book, "The Science of Getting Rich," written by Wallace D. Wattles. She captivated us with her exploration of the power of intention and the Law of Attraction. She brought together Bob Proctor and many new thought teachers and created a movie explaining the Law of Attraction and how it could be used for a better life.

I devoured "The Secret" like it was the dessert to the main course of personal growth material I had been munching on for years. I combined this new information with the lessons from PSI seminars and saw excellent results. I was alone at the time and starting to creatively imagine the perfect life partner. Once the picture was clear I released it and accepted it as done. Not more than six months later, I met the absolute love of my life. We are now married and love each other dearly. We found each other, not six months from imagination to actualization. It looked like I was finally understanding how to manifest.

Unfortunately, once again, I became frustrated. I made progress, but I was far from making a difference in the lives of others, and liberty still eluded me. I started to doubt again.

Questions popped up, such as, "It seemed to work on some things and not others, why?" or "Why is it taking so long to see results?"

Did I really attract my life partner or was that just luck?

I wrestled with those questions but continued working on myself. I did not stop searching, reading, or learning. I mixed and matched different philosophies and theories, and then it hit me. I had forgotten the auto-programming piece and the work produced by Dr. Maxwell Maltz. Once I incorporated the auto-programming part, I started gaining some traction. I began to see positive results, but the journey was far from over. There are always more things to learn.

Pop Quiz: What's the fastest way to get a new wardrobe?
Answer: Throw out all your clothes.

If you want new clothes, toss your clothes out and make room first. You will get new clothes. This was a hard lesson to learn for me. I had to clear out space for my new, better beliefs and perspectives. When you set your intention for something, you must make room and believe it is coming. Doubt must never, never, never enter the equation, or all forward motion halts. The Law of Attraction is always at work, and you are presently attracting the things you have now. You will keep attracting the things you have always had unless you clear out all old programs and install new ones.

It has taken nearly 20 years to figure out how to consistently manifest the things I wanted. I must warn you the long road is costly. My journey here cost me relationships, hundreds of thousands of dollars, and two companies, and my hair began thinning horribly.

However, because of my 20-year experiment, I found an extremely effective way to blend multiple modalities for personal growth, personal and business success into one holistic system. It will work for anyone, even those who are profoundly analytical and take a little longer to catch on. In this book, I will introduce this process to you that helped me to take control of my income and my life. I take great joy in showing you how you can accomplish this too. When you set your mind, you can select your life. I am not saying that it will be easy. Life is always throwing you curve balls, but armed with your tools you can weather any storm.

This book will help you better understand how to live intentionally, acquire, and maintain the correct mindset and raise your vibration to the energy of the person who has already achieved the goal. Then your subconscious mind will do the rest. I hope you become inspired to work on yourself and seek a community and mentor.

It is said when the student is ready, the teacher will appear. Ask yourself, Are you ready?

Introduction

"The road to success is always under construction."
-Lily Tomlin

Everything that we see, touch, or perceive is energy. I will explain the Law of Attraction and energy later in the book. Still, the takeaway is that everything in your life is there because you attract it. The Law of Attraction is always at work; it does not rest. What you attract is controlled by your self-image and your unconscious programming. I became aware of this in my teens. My circumstances, which I will share later, forced me to analyze my programs early in life. I found that you can never be greater than your self-image and will never operate outside of your current programming unless you consciously choose to. Suppose your present circumstances are not to your liking. In that case, you need to identify what you hold as your self-image and up-level it. Simultaneously it would help if you upgraded the programs you are running. Most of the programs were planted into your mind during your youth. I will go into that in more detail later.

This book details my experiences and A-Ha moments going from ignorance to inspiration and results. We have all embarked on a journey, and at the end of the day, we have one thing in common. It is to be happy, connected, helpful to others, and enjoy some measure of success. Many of us become confused along the way. The secret to creating a successful, joy-filled life is to "know thy self." This book provides a foundation to begin that journey and explains the tools I used to create from pure intention.

Part I of this book, Tools, is an introduction to powerful tools and philosophies available for creating the life we choose. We cover intention, attraction, and manifesting. I reverence many of the leading experts on these topics. Many of my clients have remarked that the way I explained these topics was simpler to grasp and the tools I use more applicable to their lives. I hope after reading that you.

Part II, Application, dives into the holistic success system I used to reprogram and ultimately overcome negative thinking, doubt, old defense mechanisms, and an inaccurate self-image. Being the stereotypical doubting Thomas, I approached everything with skepticism. I was a hard nut to crack and found no one system worked for me; there are many. So, I took what worked from many available techniques and built my own. This section will provide an overview and insight into the Laser Focus Success system. The process starts with a sincere desire to take charge of your life and honest introspection. Psychologists believe most of the subconscious programs running our lives were installed by the time we were eight. With new insights, we can break the chains of an outdated self-image, old programs, and defense mechanisms. Shining the light on and acknowledging old programs or an inaccurate self-image will give the clarity needed to remove and replace them. Then we can fully actualize our path and our best life.

In Part III, Reflections, I share philosophies, observations, and results. Using the Law of Attraction, I created opportunities out of nothing.

I failed like everybody, but eventually I figured it out. If you have tried and failed to bring your dreams to life, pat yourself on the back because you have done more than 90% of the population. Don't give up. Failure is a necessary step in the quest for anything. Failure provides an opportunity to reflect. Ask yourself whether this was due to some outside circumstance or if this is an internal issue that you need to work on? It is like the kiln that fires "the clay" into beautiful pottery. You grow from every failure into a person that can accomplish anything. If you understand the tools at your disposal and commit to improving daily, they will help you move toward a fulfilling life. I recommend that you shorten your journey and find a coach or mentor. Without guidance and accountability, your doubts and subconscious programs have the upper hand. I delayed my results by overanalyzing everything and not seeking advice. I was suffering from analysis paralysis. I finally forced myself to take action and create the successful system that I share with you in this book. Laser Focus is a multi-purpose process that addresses the most critical thing common to any situation, business or personal, you.

To learn more about Laser Focus or to inquire about coaching, send an email to tsolivaresbooks@gmail.com

facebook.com/thomas.olivares.771/

PART I: Tools

"Reflection is one the most underused yet powerful tool for success."
-Richard Carlson

Everything is a tool for the mind. If you look at meditation, for example. We quiet our minds. We turn off the outside noise, and we focus the mind inward. When we recite affirmations or listen to a new concept or teaching, we expand our understanding and belief within our minds. You can say everything is "in" your mind. What we focus on expands.

Meditation, affirmations and auto-programming, sound therapy, hypnosis, tapping, counting and NLP are just a few of the modalities available for creating changes in how we operate and what we believe. Some processes require little actions, rituals, and specific movements. These actions act as signals and provide reinforcement and programming, so the mind knows what is coming next. The outside world provides a constant distraction. We must use tools to help the mind see past the distraction to the truth within. Everyone is different, and not every tool will work for everyone. Some people swear by tapping, and others feel hypnotherapy works better. Some like guided meditation, and others prefer a vision quest. Your job is to choose the ones that work for you. That is more challenging than it sounds and can become like a game of whack-a-mole. If you attempt to use a tool and find you are not reaching your objective, you must stand firm that the goal is reachable and accept that you have just selected the wrong tool. Choose again. Many give up at this point. I played whack-a-mole for a while, but I stuck it out, and the "end result" is a process I call Laser Focus.

Attraction, Intention, Mind, and Focus are at our disposal. The Laser Focus system, explained in a later chapter, is the blend of tools that focus the mind. Meditations, goal setting and life scripting are standard practices used by many coaches and mentors. We add the use of emotions and the five senses in the envisioning process. The training incorporates wisdom and teachings from pioneers like Thomas Willhite, Neville Goddard, Napoleon Hill, Wallace D Wattle, Dr. Wayne Dyer, Bob Proctor, and many others. Nothing is new or untried, only recombined in a new way. My mission is to assist people in removing their own self-imposed cages and reaching their full potential. We were created to do remarkable things and to lift each other up. Let's be exceptional.

Chapter One: Intention

"Intention is a force in the universe, and everything and everyone is connected to this invisible force. "
-Dr. Wayne Dyer

Intention is an internal driving force and the unseen hand that brings your goals and dreams to life. Intention works hand in hand with attraction.

Merriam and Webster and the Oxford Dictionaries define Intention as follows:

1. What one intends to do or bring about…

2. The object for which a prayer, mass, or pious act is offered.

3. A determination to act a certain way; with resolve

Dr. Wayne Dyer produced a fantastic body of work in his study of Intention. In his 2004 book "The power of intention," Wayne explains that the connection to Intention is very much like a connection to a higher mind. It's as if some unseen hand is putting all the pieces in place.

Another catchphrase I learned from PSI seminars is "When the Intention is Clear, the Mechanism Will Appear." This axiom dovetails very nicely with Dr. Dyer's definition. Both agree that if you apply all your focus and energy to your intention, you need not worry about the mechanism, opportunity, or tool required to achieve your goal. It will make itself known in due time. Intention brings about a remarkable concurrence of events or circumstances without apparent causal connection. These events are commonly referred to as coincidences. It is a complex series of events that transpire, leaving you in awe, attempting to figure out how it could happen that way.

Dr. Maxwell Maltz also weighs in on the topic. He suggests the subconscious mind is connected to some unknown force. In his book Psycho-Cybernetics, he cites numerous experiences where the creative mechanism in the brain would have access to a universal mind. All religions and spiritual practices concur there is a superconscious mind, the mind of the Universe, of God, to which we are all connected. There is quite a consensus on this topic.

Chapter Two: Attraction

"By visualizing your goal already complete, you flip your mind onto the frequency that contains the way that it will be attracted to you."
-Bob Proctor

The Law of Attraction states that positive thoughts will bring positive results, and negative thoughts will bring negative ones. The law is more like a philosophy than an actual law. It is a description of an activity; it is an observation. It is not a physical law like the Law of Gravity, yet just like the Law of Gravity, it operates whether you are aware of it or not. This attraction philosophy is built on a sound basis. Everything that exists is energy in motion. Particles of a similar frequency attract each other, while different frequencies repel. Their properties are based on the laws of physics. Higher vibrational frequencies are associated with positive or healthy expression states. Lower ones have been measured with sadness, unhealthy cells, and cancer. We perceive this energy in the forms of solid, liquid, and gas. The different presentations of energy are due to the rate of speed, vibrational frequency, and intensity. Massive planets and our sun are just huge expressions of energy. The sun and planets are attracted to each other and revolve around each other, exhibiting the same properties as a microscopic Atom with its nucleus and electrons field. The heavenly bodies are the most significant expression of energy we currently perceive. We can see how attraction works on a grand scale. Yet, it can be challenging to acknowledge attraction on a micro-scale without access to a super-powered microscope or testing equipment. On a non-visible or super micro-scale, we can measure the effects our thoughts, imaginations, feelings, and emotions have on us. While certain states of reflection or emotion are being experienced, the vibratory frequencies within our cells and brains can be measured by sensitive equipment.

Slowly I changed my programs, and the life I observed changed. Remember, observing the wave in physics creates the particle that makes up reality. We are participants in our life, but first, we are the observers. To correct what we observe, we must first change our thoughts. Just like you, I am still challenged by things life brings my way, but now I can always find the lesson or the silver lining, and my joy is always with me. It would be my pleasure to help you experience your life the same way. Please enjoy the last few sections of insights, discoveries, and results.

Happy thoughts will register at a specific vibrational frequency, while unhappy thoughts will register at a different lower frequency. The body's resonant frequencies can also be measured. Healthy cells resonate at a frequency of 62-70 MHz! Frequencies of 58 MHz or lower have been measured when someone is sick or otherwise infirmed. Frequencies identified in patients with cancer were predominantly found in the 1000Hz range. Everything, even thought, and emotion, has a vibrational frequency. If vibrational frequency dictates attraction, altering our thoughts and feelings will naturally affect what we attract. Thoughts are powerful things. Everything humanity has created first existed in mind. The thought of a rocket ship was science fiction until it was made manifest through intention and the creative powers of humanity. With the proper use of the mind, intention, imagination, and emotion discussed later in the book, you will see how to progressively drive the things you want into your life.

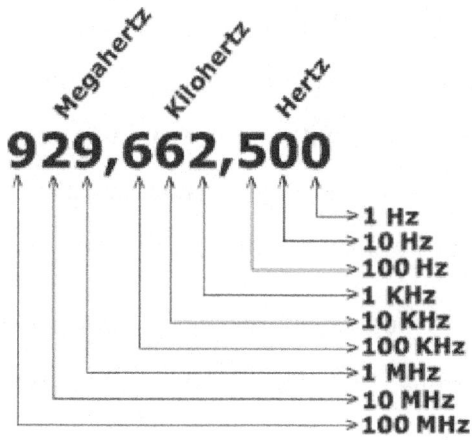

Chapter Three: The Mind
"All Problems Are Illusions of The Mind."
-Eckhart Tolle

Locked up in our subconscious (mind/brain) is an unbelievable machine that has controlled our outward experience since we were born. What we truly believe about ourselves, and the world will dictate how we experience reality. We must recognize that our perception of reality is governed by our senses and filters. In Physics, we learn that an electron is only a wave until it is observed. A wave is a disturbance that travels through a medium, transporting energy from one location (its source) to another without transporting matter. Only after being observed does a wave become a particle. A particle is a physical thing we can count. This means the observer creates reality.

The Athenian philosopher Plato (c. 427-347 B.C.) influenced western philosophy by developing several of its branches: epistemology, metaphysics, ethics, and aesthetics. He asserts "that the physical world around us is not real. It is constantly changing; thus, you can never say what it really is. There is a world of ideas which is a world of unchanging and absolute truth." We experience reality through electrical impulses we receive with our senses. These impulses are then translated by our brains. Each person interprets those signals through the filters of their beliefs, self-image and how they perceive they fit in the world. The world is not absolute; it changes based on the filters we have stored in our minds. When you wake up in the morning, it is you and your thoughts. You are the center of your universe. The world is produced by the unconscious thoughts in your mind. Most have yet to be made aware of this fact. How do you greet your world? Many find the world a pleasant, wonderful place and welcome their new day with a smile, some live in fright. It is the same world, yet the experience of it is different.

Here is a simple example. Someone who is not challenged when seeing a spider will look upon the spider on the wall with little concern. However, someone afraid of spiders will see it and find their heart rate climbing, their palms sweaty, and they may even scream. That represents different experiences of the same world at the same time. The experience is controlled by the programs running in the mind. We need to analyze the programs and unconscious thoughts to make this change. The process begins with honest inventory of our core beliefs and self-image. This is a culmination of all the things we accepted about the self and our world. Most of the things we believe were installed in our minds by others a long time ago. Psychologists believe that what our parents think about the world becomes transferred to us by age eight. We were too young to question what we were told. Most are unaware of the programs, so they remain unchecked and unchanging. Our relationships shape us as well. Some relationships are nurturing, some are destructive, and all have an impact. This honest inventory can explain how we created our current life circumstances. It can also point to the adjustments necessary to shift to the life we want. Our parents did the best they could. Most of them knew very little about the Law of Attraction and the power of intention. It is time to challenge these stored beliefs. Today, we are fortunate that many brilliant thinkers have cracked the code to co-create our lives. The philosophies are sound and well-explained, and there are countless success stories of those who dared to believe "they" could be more. Pioneers like Napoleon Hill, Wallace D. Wattles, Neville, Goddard, Dr. Wayne Dyer, Dr. Maxwell Maltz, Anthony Robbins, and Bob Proctor, to name only a few, postulated, tested, and shared their success in the arena of personal growth and the creative powers of man. We are no longer doomed to the beliefs we accepted as a truth long before we could judge for ourselves. So, we take that honest personal inventory, and then we begin to reprogram our subconscious.

We must understand and practice the BE DO HAVE principle. BE in the energy and space of already achieving the goal. Envision yourself DOING the things you would do if the goal was achieved and HAVING the things the goal accomplished would make available to you. Using the imagination, you mentally take possession of the home or the car or whatever it is that the goal achieved would bring. For our divinely inspired subconscious mechanism to work, our goal must be conceived as "already in existence now." Dr. Maxwell Maltz argues that the goal must be accepted, as already done. In Psycho-Cybernetics, he writes, "The means by which your Success Mechanism works often take care of themselves and do so effortlessly when you supply the goal to your brain. The precise steps will come to you without stress, tension, or worry about how you are going to accomplish the result you seek."

Chapter Four: Focus

"The Secret of Change Is To Focus All of Your Energy Not On Fighting The Old, But On Building The New."
-Socrates

A laser is uniquely powerful and versatile at the same time. It can use focused rays of light to correct the curvature of the eye and cut through steel like it was butter. The result is ultimately dependent on the focus.

Merriam-Webster defines focus as a point of concentration. "Directed" attention: emphasis.

Like the laser, intention is amplified by focus. Focused intention is the key to raising your vibration and what you attract. As we embark on self-growth, we must start with an inward focus. We must take responsibility for our lives and what we believe and have created. We become more aware of ourselves during this process, leading to a focus on others. We realize that the life we experience reflects what we believe, and everyone is part of that reflection. We become a focused self-leader. The judging of everything incorrectly stops, and we find value in all our experiences. Many of which we create to teach or show ourselves something we need to learn. The journey becomes more pleasant. We begin to experience appreciation and gratitude. We move from a focused self-leader to "Focused Leadership," and we start to show others the way. Daniel Goleman, author of "The Focused Leader," explains leaders need to cultivate a triad of awareness — an inward focus, a focus on others, and an outward focus.

This outward focus will raise your vibration. When we intentionally focus on positive thoughts, feelings, and emotions, we naturally begin to act in gratitude. Gratitude, one of the highest vibrations, is always accompanied by an internal sense of joy. Joy is one of life's greatest gifts and allows you to be content in any circumstance. Remember, the Law of Attraction will cause us to attract things and outcomes with vibrations that match ours. Need I say more?

PART II: APPLICATION

"Inspiration and information without personal application never amount to transformation."
-Lysa TerKeurst

The best way to enlightenment does not exist, nor is there one best teacher or coach. At least not alive today. I have learned from many of the gurus and top coaches. I have digested the training and philosophies of most of the bestselling authors in the personal growth genre. Each one imparted something significant to me. Yet none gave me everything I needed to consistently manifest my goals. I am an analyst, remember, and I needed more data. They often left out something. I believe in focusing on the positives, but I am one who likes to know the pitfalls and the things I should avoid. I should have enlisted the help of a mentor. A mentor teaches, but they will also guide you based on their experience. They will help you see your choices and what you should avoid. As coincidence would have it, I was guided to find those missing bits of information and the right mentor. As if some unseen figure or hand knew my need and filled it. That is the mystery of this thing called life.

The journey was long but immensely rewarding. It enabled me to create a process, a way to apply the knowledge and technique I can share with others. This system is modeled after the methods I used to manifest the lifestyle I wanted. There is nothing new; all the tools are currently used worldwide by different coaches and teachers. I have my own take on the process. My life is not perfect, and I still have ups and downs. Just because you find some enlightenment doesn't mean the struggle goes away. It just changes.

To help others, I decided to share my process, understanding of universal laws, and the powers of the human mind and spirit. I moved past my limiting beliefs and am passionate about helping others do the same things. I am constantly learning and adding stuff as I do.

Chapter Five: Laser Focus
"Focus like a laser not a flashlight."
-Michael Jordan

Laser Focus is what I use to describe my success system. It is an acronym that cleverly speaks to the process and the outcome.

Process:

Locate self-image, self-talk conversations and unconscious, unproductive programs.

Auto-program by properly feeding the success mechanism that is the subconscious mind and practicing gratitude.

Suspend disbelief and doubts with active thought control scripting and recordings.

Engage the process for at least 21 days.

Review, Revise and Repeat.

Outcome:

Format and

Organize your

Conscious thinking and

Uniting it with your

Subconscious success system.

The tools selected are based on the participant. The methods and the tools I chose helped me to stay focused. It effectively eliminated the contrarian voice that lived in my head for as long as I can remember. I was able to experience better, more consistent communication between my conscious and subconscious minds. I now enjoy what I call inspired thoughts, which seem to come from a higher mind than mine. We all get off track and lose focus, but, with little hacks, audios, specific memorized scripts, and affirmations, it was easy to refocus quickly.

The work starts with identifying and acknowledging outdated and self-destructive thought patterns that prevent us from achieving the results we are looking to create. We then build new evidence, internal conversations, practices, and beliefs. Combining traditional learning modalities with emotions, envisioning, and "as if achieved" intention goal setting allows the subconscious mind to do what it does best.

This system incorporates all 5 learning modalities creating a layered effect. Daily practices include writing, reading, listening, speaking, imagining, and envisioning. Once put in place, it involves short activities scattered throughout the day. I use a holistic approach to goal setting, which addresses life's physical, emotional, social, spiritual, and intellectual aspects. A balanced approach is more nurturing to the soul. We were never meant to be alone as a species. This program seeks to support the participant in being part of a community or, in today's terminology, a tribe. An accountability partner is also recommended.

Life's external circumstances have a significant effect on our efforts. To address this, I reference Maslow's hierarchy of human needs to gauge motivation. Abraham Maslow was an American psychologist who developed a hierarchy of needs to explain human motivation. His theory suggested that people have a few basic requirements that must be met before people move up the hierarchy to pursue more social, emotional, and self-actualizing needs. Ultimately, the goal is to reach the top of the pyramid and help others do the same.

Self-actualization
desire to become the most that one can be

Esteem
respect, self-esteem, status, recognition, strength, freedom

Love and belonging
friendship, intimacy, family, sense of connection

Safety needs
personal security, employment, resources, health, property

Physiological needs
air, water, food, shelter, sleep, clothing, reproduction

Chapter Six: How to Begin
"Making the beginning is one third of the work."
-Irish Proverb

The first step is to collect data. The Personal Inventory template starts with a series of questions that allows you to write down your thoughts upon waking and before sleep. The things you say or think to yourself when you look in the mirror. What do you think about when you are not thinking? These answers are not good or bad, information is neutral. We place a value and a meaning on it with our filters. We challenge our filters through other exercises. Refrain from judging the answers and be completely honest. We can begin to see patterns; some are awesome and serve us. Many are the very things standing in our way. With this information, we can identify the source code. It was eye-opening when I looked at how I operated and reacted to the circumstances in my life. The most crucial step was to look extreme honesty.

The gratefulness exercise gives us a chance to put life into perspective. If we consider someone whose circumstances have left them homeless, we can be grateful we are not. Many of our fellow humans have been born into poverty, and we should give thanks every day if we have not. Some are stricken with conditions that prevent them from walking or holding a job; we should be grateful again that we are not. Many are one paycheck away from bankruptcy. Often, we cannot see through the illusion that looking good portrays. The Law of Attraction will only work if you practice extreme gratitude and many attempts to use the law fail for this one reason.

Then you envision your perfect future. Dream big, and do not worry about how you will achieve it. Your subconscious mind will ultimately do the work. We then focus on challenging but achievable goals for growing your life, building, or scaling your business, etc. This builds confidence and creates a positive feedback loop. Finding the why comes next. We use a drill-down process that helps to clarify the core of the goal. The "Why" is the fuel that amplifies your focused intention! In the drill-down process, you will realize that there are two types of goals. Means and ends. A means goal could be to make 1,000,000 dollars. Money should never be confused with your Ends goal. It is more like a tool or mechanism.

The Ends goal is the why. An Ends goal may be that you promised your mother, who worked tirelessly to provide for you and your siblings, that you would buy her a house and take care of her in her golden years. The feeling and emotions connected to your Ends goals are unbelievably powerful. That needs to be where we focus. Then you envision your perfect future. Dream big, and do not worry about how you will achieve it. Your subconscious mind will ultimately do the work. We then focus on challenging but achievable goals that represent action steps into the unknown. We must not try to be perfect; we improve and learn by taking imperfect "action." This builds confidence and creates a positive feedback loop. Remember doing nothing yields nothing. Making mistakes brings about learning.

We follow that by taking a hard look at the cognitive distortions. These usually develop over time in response to adverse events. This exercise helps us address the programs that are running in our subconscious minds. Unless addressed they will wreak havoc and keep us from reaching our true potential.

We lose information through "Generalizations", "Deletion" of information and "Cognitive Distortion". Distortion is where some aspects of ideas and experiences are given more weight and focus than others. We all do this both consciously and unconsciously, and how we do this provides pointers to our underlying beliefs about ourselves, others, and the world. Cognitive distortions become our habitual way of thinking, often inaccurate and negatively biased. Once you identify an unproductive behavior, you can choose differently.

Another essential tool for calling our future into existence is the creation of a Life Script. A life script is a forward-looking document to speak the future into reality. It contains statements about the things we are attracting into our lives. It integrates the things that are identified in the gratefulness exercise. There are many ways we employ this script to create maximum subconscious buy-in. I have included some samples below. This process works better with a guide. If you need someone to guide and support you on this journey, write to me at

tsolivaresbooks@gmail.com

Chapter Seven: The Inventory

"Don't kid yourself. Be honest with yourself. Take your own inventory."
-Jack Canfield

Below I share with you a few sample questions.

Do you greet the day with enthusiasm? If not, how do you?
_____
_____

What are your first thoughts upon waking?
_____
_____

What is your last thought before sleep comes?
_____
_____

When you look in the mirror what is your first thought, what do you say to yourself?
_____
_____

Is silence challenging? _____

Do you need a radio playing to drown out your thoughts?
_____

What are those thoughts?
_____
_____

Chapter Eight: Gratefulness
"Gratitude turns what we have into enough."
–Aesop

Practicing gratitude helps to create a HABIT where we focus on the positive side of life. Write down all the things you are grateful for and be very detailed. Include things like clean air and a healthy body, water, family, etc.

_____
_____
_____
_____
_____
_____
_____
_____
_____
_____
_____
_____
_____
_____
_____

Chapter Nine: The Future
"The best way to predict the future is to create it."
-Abraham Lincoln

Look three years into the future. What is your ideal life and do not think about how you will create it. Just fantasize. How much are you making, who is with you and what your perfect day looks like? What kind of car do you drive, what color is it and does it have heated seats. Take a minute and imagine it first and then jot down everything you see. The more specific the better.

_____
_____
_____
_____
_____
_____
_____
_____
_____
_____
_____
_____
_____
_____

Chapter Ten: Picking Your Goals
"A goal without a plan is only a dream."
-Brian Tracy

Let's set goals that will bring that dream life into view. There are three types of goals. Goals we already know how to accomplish, we have done them before, like a new car. There are goals that we do not know how to accomplish but we are pretty sure we can figure it out. This might be becoming the captain of a fishing ship. Then there are goals so big that we have no idea how we would even start. These are called fantasy goals. We have a twenty-one-step process for identifying the goals that align with your purpose and passion. We SMART goal setting technique.

GREAT Goals are:

Outcome focused: Once you understand your WHY (and it's an enthusiastic WHY) you're 90% there!

In line with your values: The more a goal aligns with your inner or core values - the EASIER it will be to achieve.

Stated in the positive: i.e. "I want healthy fingernails" rather than "I want to stop biting my nails."

SMART:

Specific (so you know exactly what you're trying to achieve)

Measurable (so you know when you've achieved it!)

Action-oriented (so you can DO something about it!)

Realistic (so it IS achievable) and Relevant to your why!

Time-Bound (has a deadline!)

Chapter Eleven: Cognitive Distortions
"If the doors of perfection were cleansed, everything would appear to man as it is, infinite."
-William Blake

Here are a few examples:

All or Nothing Thinking: Seeing things as black-or-white, right-or-wrong with nothing in between. Essentially, if I'm not perfect then I'm a failure.
- I didn't finish writing that paper, so it was a *complete* waste of time.
- There's no point in playing *if I'm not 100%* in shape.
- They didn't show, they're *completely* unreliable!

Overgeneralization: Using words like always, never in relation to a single event or experience.
- I'll *never* get that promotion.
- She *always* does that…

Minimizing or Magnifying (Also Catastrophizing): Seeing things as dramatically more or less important than they "actually" are. Often creating a "catastrophe" that follows.

- *Because* my boss publicly thanked her, she'll get that promotion, not me (even though I had a great performance review and just won an industry award).
- I forgot that email! *That means* my boss won't trust me again, I won't get that raise and my wife will leave me.

"Shoulds": Using "should", "need to", "must", "ought to" to motivate oneself, then feeling guilty when you don't follow through (or anger and resentment when someone else doesn't follow through).
- *I should have* got the painting done this weekend.
- *They ought to* have been more considerate of my feelings, *they should know* that would upset me.

Labelling: Attaching a negative label to yourself or others following a single event.
- I didn't stand up to my co-worker, *I'm such a whim.*
- *What an idiot,* he couldn't even see that coming!

Chapter Twelve: Life Script
"You define your own life. Don't let other people write your script."
-Oprah Winfrey

The life script will incorporate your goals and things written down in the gratefulness exercise. All statements must be presented in the context of already possessed, achieved, or "attracting." The idea is to express gratitude toward all the items you presently have and those you are still attracting.

An example would be: "I am so happy and grateful that I am in perfect health. Each night, I sleep peacefully while my body is restored and refreshed. I am grateful for the water and sunshine that fuels the plants in my garden. I am grateful that I can nourish my body with the clean food I am growing and that there is always enough to share with my neighbors…." (You get the idea)

The life script is the ultimate positive affirmation. It must be read, listened to, and recited multiple times daily.

Chapter Thirteen: The Routine
"The secret of your future is hidden in your daily routine."
-Mike Murdock

Everyone's routine will be a bit different. It must fit into your life. Too many programs are set around timetables and contain activities that do not blend with your life. If it is too intrusive, you will not follow through. You must commit to your growth because no one can do it for you. The system aims to understand your lifestyle and to integrate with it.

This routine will include all learning modalities described in an earlier section. They include reading, writing, speaking, hearing, and imagining. We also incorporate the use of your five senses. Some of us learn better when we watch a video, some of us need to read, and others benefit most when they write. We also incorporate visualizations, relaxation, meditation, centering exercises, and creative imagining. Everything is energy, and the idea is to move the energy in as many ways as possible.

The mind understands pictures better than words. Let me give you an example. When you read or hear the phrase, "do not think of a purple elephant," everybody sees a purple elephant. The mind couldn't do anything with the word not or don't. It is for that reason we always focus on the things we want to see, create or receive. The subconscious mind requires repetition. At least twenty-one days are needed to plant a new habit, but it does not end there. The mind is like a muscle, it needs to be challenged, or it will get sluggish and fall back to old habits. For example, you pick up a fifteen-pound weight. Not heavy but not light either. You start to curl it. You can do three sets of twenty reps, and you will do those two or three times a week. By week three, it feels light, so you pick up the twenty-pounder and repeat the process. You're strong enough to do twenty pounds. Now lay off the weight training for two or three weeks. When you return, that twenty-pound weight feels heavy, so you return to fifteen-pound weights to work your way up again. That is how the mind works too. So, our routine will change to continue to challenge our minds and support continued growth.

The most crucial part of the routine is gratitude. It is impossible to complain and be grateful at the same time. Complaining focuses on lack and comes with negative thoughts. We know that negative thoughts will provide negative results. That is why we place all the things we are grateful for in our life script. This keeps up in high vibration. The mind will eventually believe the statements in your life script. As previously explained, the subconscious will do all the work. The mind cannot tell reality from a dream. Have you ever woken up in a pool of sweat because of an awful dream? The events didn't really happen, but the body reacted as if it did. Repetition is the key to auto-programming, and the conversation we have with ourselves is the program.

You can apply the Laser Focus process to building or growing your business, becoming healthier, or finding a life partner. Self-mastery is a lifelong journey that is worth every minute you invest.

PART III: REFLECTIONS

"Learning without reflection is a waste. Reflection without learning is dangerous."
-Confucius

This section of the book is unstructured, so I may communicate a variety of things with you to reflect on. I didn't share in the forward that I became a father quite young. At seventeen years of age, I became a dad and got married. By the time I was twenty-one, I was divorced and had custody of two boys. I was a single dad in the 80s when there weren't many men with custody of their children. I had no examples of how to be a single dad. I didn't know how to be what I was. My example of a dad was that of a two-parent household. My programs of parenthood would not work for me now. I was forced to look at my programs about fatherhood and day by day created a new one. This really gave birth to my lifelong search for the ideal life. I have no regrets and am grateful for the experience; I love my children.

On those nights when the boys were asleep, I would sit on the porch and watch the cars drive by. I observed other people living their lives, unsure how to live mine. Slowly I changed my programs, and the life I observed changed. Remember, observing the wave in physics creates the particle that makes up reality. We are participants in our life, but first, we are the observers. To correct what we observe, we must first change our thoughts. I, like you, are still challenged by things life brings my way, but now I can always find the lesson or the silver lining, and my joy is always with me. The quest in life, ultimately, is to find joy. It would be my pleasure to help you experience your life the same way. Please enjoy the last few sections of insights, discoveries, and results.

Surrender Early
"The ultimate act of power is surrender."
-Krishna Das

I would only recommend walking the path to Personal Growth and development with others. Find a mentor and a community you resonate with. The journey can be strange and lonely since much of the world is genuinely asleep. Your peers may need help understanding your quest for truth or enlightenment. The concept of the Law of Attraction is not new, but it sits outside of the mainstream. It continues to garner more attention than in years past, but it gets watered down to make it more palatable to the average person. The Law of Attraction was first articulated in 1886. The first pioneer to speak of the Law of Attraction as an essential principle was Prentice Mulford, an author, and humorist. He was pivotal in the development of New Thought thinking. He wrote an essay that discusses the Law of Attraction as "The Law of Success," published 1886-1887. Since then, every generation has offered some new interpretation that makes it easier to understand. Unfortunately, much of the world is unaware of how connected we all are. Everyone has a significant effect on the whole.

Today's world is in a horrible shape, mainly because everyone believes they are separate from one another. The world has forgotten that we are all connected. So many people are miserable and broken inside, but they are shiny and polished outside. Everyone must have the latest gadgets, clothes, and electronics because that is what they are told will make them happy. You are part of the solution—everyone who steps up and learns how to manifest their future tips the scale a little more. We will eventually hit a tipping point when critical mass occurs, and many will come to understand what they are capable of. Using the Law of Attraction requires faith. You must step out on a limb and believe what you cannot see. When I started this journey, I was like the rest of the world. I didn't understand how to create the life I wanted. I was an extreme analyst, believed it was possible, and never gave up.

I finally figured out that my doubt was what kept me from succeeding. Success came when I performed without a safety net. What exactly does that mean? I had to paint myself into a corner that I could only get out of if I succeeded. You may remember the story about Hernan Cortes. In 1519, he arrived in the "New World" with 600 men and, upon arrival, made history by "burning his ships." This sent a clear message to his men. There is no turning back! Two years later, he succeeded in his complete conquest of the Aztec empire. Against ridiculous odds, they succeeded because the intention was clear; there was no giving up. I gave myself only one choice to succeed, and I did, although my story is not as dramatic as Cortes'.

Another valuable lesson is that there are two ways to do things. Brute force and go with the flow or, as it is called, operate in the flow. Brute force is difficult, takes more effort, and often produces a result with less joy attached. The flow is like when Michael Jordan crosses the half-court line with the ball and knows that three points are needed to win. He flies into the air, seeming to defy gravity, and lands an impossible three-pointer, never doubting the outcome for a second. You can choose to win by fighting the current if you don't die from exhaustion or you can just turn around and let it carry you. Which way would you prefer to operate? I recommend that you find a mentor who can show you how to ride the current and surrender your disbelief early.

Unwavering Belief Required
"Miracles don't happen to you. They happen through you."
-Mary Davis

The Law of Attraction works yet not always the way we expect. I have enjoyed some amazing outcomes intentionally using this law. I have shared them in a later chapter, but I must first point out the importance of belief. The timetable to the goal achieved and mechanisms that lead us there exist outside our understanding. When I look back at some of the seemingly chance and coincidental occurrences, I am tempted to call them miracles. The Oxford dictionary defines a miracle as a surprising and welcome event that is not explicable by natural or scientific laws and is therefore considered to be the work of a divine agency. We were divinely crafted creatures, and we are endowed with the ability to create new life and a life that is worth living. Most understand how to create life, but few have been instructed as the way to make it amazing. Our subconscious mind and its connection to source does the work, and your belief is the key.

Belief must be accompanied by faith and expectancy. Setting your intention, imagining the goal as already accomplished, operating as if, and doing the work described in this book is not enough. It is vital that you remain resolute in your belief that everything will work out. This requires patience. Belief refers to something we consider true even if there is no proof. Faith is trusting someone or something from the depth of our hearts. Finally, we must embody a childlike expectancy comparable to how a young child beams on Christmas Eve knowing that Santa is on his way. Doubt must never be allowed to enter your thoughts. It will poison the water and make your journey longer. Be unwavering!

The Poison and the Antidote
"The best antidote for fear is knowledge."
-Robin S. Sharma

Repetition is the indispensable tool that allows us to reprogram and change the thoughts that seem to fire off in our minds automatically. Even with the best efforts and intention I was frequently caught off-guard in the morning when I woke up. My experiences proved to me that this is the easiest time of the day for the old thoughts and seeds of doubt to seep in, like drops of poison. In the early stage, we begin to wall off and move the old programs, insecurities, and doubts into cold storage. We do that by creating a new internal conversation. This new body of thoughts begins to expand and make a home. When we are full of energy, focused, and engaged with our new beliefs, it is as if there is a guard on duty blocking old programs. These old programs are inactive but pieces of them always remain. When we get tired, the guard falls asleep. Old thoughts begin to linger. When we recognize this happening, we need to use our affirmations and scripts to quiet the chatter.

In the morning upon returning from the dreamscape, we may find that the brain isn't firing yet, and our thought guard has yet to wake up. This is when a hint of doubt or the poison of insecurity has the best chance of taking advantage of the situation. I had that problem and finally solved it by always having the antidote nearby. The recorded version of the life script is your antidote. Put in an earphone and start playing the recorded life script over and over again. I would close my eyes and watch the poison recede and clarity return. This solution was a game changer. Anyone inspired to start a new life, venture, or relationship is entering a scary space. These tools work for any goal or purpose. Old programs will always pop up, but you will have the antidote ready when they do.

Big Goals – Little Goals

"Your goal should be out of reach, but not out of sight."
-Denis Waitley and Remi Witt

Have you ever wondered why it takes so long to manifest some things and almost no time to create others when using intention and the Law of Attraction? Attracting or manifesting something significant, like a fantasy goal (big and you have no idea how to achieve it), will take longer than small ones. In most cases, more extensive plans involve other people, free will, and many moving parts. There is no way to even guess the timeline, but bigger things will take more time.

Conversely, suppose you have a few smaller goals where you are the primary driver of activity. I am not talking about things you know how to do. These goals are slightly out of reach, and there is still some uncertainty about how or if you will hit the target. When correctly using intention, we bear witness to coincidences and unexplained synchronicities. That is because an unseen agent is at work. This is the energy that you are directing toward the goal.

To help you understand this effect and the concept of energy, I will refer to studies performed on Random Number Generators (RNG). An RNG is a computer program that generates random numbers. To generate PRNGs, a computer uses a seed number and an algorithm to generate numbers that seem random but are predictable. Subjects observed and attempted to influence the results. In these tests, an observer was shown to have a small but measurable effect on the results. The results deviated slightly from those predicted. Unfortunately, there was no way to scientifically describe or explain the agent or mechanism that caused the deviation, so the studies were declared inconclusive. The energetic world is subtle, as seen in the slight deviation, but at the same time, mighty as we use it to create the world.

Results
"You can have results or excuses not."
-Arnold Schwarzenegger

Throughout my life, I enjoyed success in every field I entered. I created several job opportunities out of nothing. I attribute every success to intention, the Law of Attraction, and my higher power, which I call God. Like many of you, I was programmed during childhood and made decisions based on what others thought. When the time came to find a career, I didn't know what I would enjoy doing for the rest of my life. Add to that a turbulent economy and fast-changing world; it's no wonder many of us find our true profession late in life. One thing I knew was that I enjoyed helping others. My father died when I was twenty-one. He did not have a lot of life insurance, and my mom had to take on a house cleaning job to make ends meet. Dad's death made such an emotional impact on me that I decided to become an insurance agent to help people be protected. I got my insurance license and started with Metropolitan Life insurance Company.

After a brief stint working as a captive agent, I created an opportunity with a small independent insurance agency struggling to generate sales. I proposed they hire me to increase their sales. I promised to bring in $30,000 monthly in a new volume on a small draw. By month four, I was generating close to $50,000 a month for this company. I was Vice President of Life and Health Insurance sales before realizing that coaching and training are what I enjoyed.

I left insurance in 1999 to start a career focused on coaching and helping others. I obtained my Certification and became a Master Personal Trainer. I worked at Bally Total Fitness and LA Fitness. I excelled as a trainer and decided that corporate life wasn't for me. I left and built a thriving private training practice, first in Georgia and again in San Diego. The business was going well until it was severely impacted by the 2008 financial crisis, which began with cheap credit and lax lending standards that fueled a housing bubble. When the bubble burst, the banks were left holding trillions of dollars of worthless investments in subprime mortgages. The Great Recession that followed cost "many" their jobs, savings, and homes. Many of my customers were affected, and I had to close my training company.

With this economic downturn, my only choice was to reinvent myself. I looked and found that solar was trending. Since I found joy in service and the economy prevented me from serving people, I would do my part to preserve the planet and our natural resources. I set my intention and accepted it as done.

While getting gas, I ended up conversing with a guy in a pickup truck. He handed me a flyer from his company, a small electrical contractor. The power of intention proved itself again. With the building industry slowing to a halt, they shifted their focus to solar and struggled to gain market share. I knew I could help them in so many ways. I called the owner and he agreed to meet. I learned that the contractor was interested in solar cleaning. He had no money in the budget to hire me. So, I proposed that I would build a solar panel cleaning division, and they could pay me when it was in place, and we became profitable. I would go on to work with this company for more than five years. After upgrading their project management systems, CRM, operations, website, and social media, I shifted to managing residential solar installations. I went to school nights and became a Certified Project Management Professional. When I started, the company had sales in the hundreds of thousands. When I left years later, they were a multimillion-dollar company with a Better Business Bureau Torch Award for Ethics tucked in their belt. Just another example of a job created out of nothing except.

I didn't worry about what I needed to know to accomplish the goal. The mechanism will appear when the intention is clear, and it always did. I was only sometimes aware of the means that brought me success. Still, in hindsight and with clarity, I see that it resulted from intention, the Law of Attraction, and my version mindset and self-programming tools. The tools became Laser Focus.

You may use the Laser Focus process to accomplish anything. Ultimately you are working on yourself. It doesn't matter if you are looking for the perfect partner or the liberty to bless others abundantly and live life on your own terms; the process works.

Joy and the Ego

"I slept and dreamt that life was joy. I awoke and saw that life was service. I acted and behold, service was joy."
-Tagore

Joy represents a high vibrational state. Joy is not achieved by acquiring things. The quest for a better life, a better job, a life partner, or million dollars is really a quest for joy. These goals are worthy, but many people feel they will find joy when they get this or accomplish that. These items will never fill you up. You will continue to search outside of yourself until you realize that joy springs from within. The challenge to finding joy can be found in our ego, self-image, and the defense mechanism we created in our youth to protect ourselves. Remember those programs that were installed by the time we were eight?

The ego is responsible for sorting out what is real. It helps us make sense of our thoughts and the world around us. Suppose the internal thinking or the self-image is inaccurate. In that case, we will have difficulty sorting out what is real and what is not. The ego is supposed to protect us from the danger of the world around us. At the dawn of man, it kept us alive. It taught us that we were separate from the world. There were things to fear and creatures that could harm us.

Today, survival instinct still exists, along with older programming, and many still operate with an unnecessary sense of fear. This only serves to separate us from each other. When we clear away and replace the old, programmed thinking with what we now know to be accurate, we replace fear with love. If we observe our world with love, we begin to experience joy. Like gratitude, living in a state of joy allows you to be content in every circumstance. You can find value and purpose within any event you encounter in life. Like a fine wine, it pairs well and is usually found in the company of bliss and happiness. Joy is the feeling experienced by one who gives and requires nothing in return, who takes pleasure in lifting up a fellow human. We all have the same creator and putting a smile on the face of another is a priceless gift for all. It is more satisfying than anything money can buy. It is the key to good health and is absent from the sick and infirmed. Just as the world reflects an inner condition, the body is that reflection. Inner turmoil will present itself as a physical condition.

It is written that those who refresh others will be refreshed. Many search their whole life for joy in their exterior landscape; no matter what they acquire, joy remains elusive. That is because joy is something you embody. The thoughts you think are responsible for creating love and joy in your world.

To learn more about Laser Focus or to inquire about coaching, send an email to tsolivaresbooks@gmail.com

For more info visit Facebook at:

facebook.com/thomas.olivares.771/

Epilogue
"Reasoning draws a conclusion, but does not make the conclusion certain, unless the mind discovers it by the path of experience."
-Roger Bacon

You Only Have Control of Your Now.

Thank you for taking the time to read this guidebook to "understanding" the tools of personal growth and how you can use them to create your life. I have explained how my program works and the tools that have brought me closer to the finish line. I am still training, writing, and learning. The journey never ends. I included contact information below for those interested in learning more.

In closing, I wanted to share some wisdom from one of my mentors, Thomas D. Willhite. In his manuscript, Thomas D. Willhite, the creator of PSI Seminars, writes, "The gift of being human is the ability to separate the past, present, and future. The wise person distinguishes the past from the future and chooses to be here now." He further explains, "when you control the now, you control the future. By controlling the future, you control the past."

You cannot change the past "in" the present, nor can you know the future from the present. But by controlling the present, you directly impact the moment. And the next moment and the one after that; you are always centered on the now. Sitting in the future, you can smile as you look back at the past you created with intention.

Live each moment being completely present. When you retire for the evening, you will leave this plane. Tomorrow you will wake up in a brand-new world. One that you can control by being present. The things in your mind govern your experience of each new day. Plant good seed, water it with wisdom, gratitude, and goodwill toward others, and you will love the world you wake in every day.

T.S. Olivares

Bibliography

Maltz, M. (1960 & 2015). Psycho-Cybernetics. New York, NY: Penguin House LLC

Hill, P. (1937). Think and Grow Rich. New York, NY: Penguin House LLC

Wattle, W.D. (2019). The Science of Getting Rich: Merchant Books

Dyer. Dr. W. (2006). The Power of Intention. Vista, CA: Hay House Publications

About The Author

T. S. Olivares

Tom is a personal coach and sales trainer living in San Diego, California, with his wife and children. With a diverse background that encompasses fitness training, sales, marketing, business management, and IT technologies, he brings substantial knowledge and insight into his business coaching and personal training.

One-on-one and in group business settings, also offering virtual individual and group sessions.

To learn more about Laser Focus or to inquire about coaching, send an email to tsolivaresbooks@gmail.com

For more info visit Facebook at: facebook.com/thomas.olivares.771/

Made in the USA
Columbia, SC
15 May 2023